Christ Humbled/Christ Exalted

Christ Humbled/ Christ Exalted

by
John MacArthur, Jr.

"GRACE TO YOU"
P.O. Box 4000
Panorama City, CA   91412

© 1990 by
JOHN F. MACARTHUR, JR.

ISBN: 0-8024-5339-2

1 2 3 4 5 6 Printing/LC/Year 94 93 92 91 90

Printed in the United States of America

Contents

These Bible studies are taken from messages delivered by Pastor-Teacher John MacArthur, Jr., at Grace Community Church in Panorama City, California. These messages have been combined into a 4-tape album titled *Christ Humbled/Christ Exalted*. You may purchase this series either in an attractive vinyl cassette album or as individual cassettes. To purchase these tapes, request the album *Christ Humbled/Christ Exalted*, or ask for the tapes by their individual GC numbers. Please consult the current price list; then, send your order, making your check payable to:

The Master's Communication
P.O. Box 4000
Panorama City, CA 91412

Or call the following toll-free number:
1-800-55-GRACE

1
The Humiliation of Christ

Outline

Introduction

Lesson
I. Christ Was God (v. 6a)
  A. The Existence of Christ
  B. The Essence of Christ
    1. The interpretive issue
    2. The scriptural support
II. Christ Did Not Cling to His Equality with God (v. 6b)
III. Christ Emptied Himself (v. 7a)
  A. He Remained God
  B. He Renounced His Privileges
    1. Heavenly glory
    2. Independent authority
    3. Divine prerogatives
    4. Eternal riches
    5. A favorable relationship
IV. Christ Became a Servant (v. 7b)
  A. A Servant by Nature
  B. A Servant by Position
V. Christ Identified with Sinners (v. 7c)
VI. Christ Looked Like a Man (v. 8a)
VII. Christ Humbled Himself (v. 8b)
VIII. Christ Was Obedient to the Point of Death (v. 8c)
IX. Christ Died on a Cross (v. 8d)

Conclusion

Introduction

Philippians 2:5-8 says, "Have this attitude in yourselves which was also in Christ Jesus, who, although He existed in the form of God, did not regard equality with God a thing to be grasped, but emptied Himself, taking the form of a bond-servant, and being made in the likeness of men. And being found in appearance as a man, He humbled Himself by becoming obedient to the point of death, even death on a cross."

A number of years ago British author C. S. Lewis wrote a book he titled *Miracles*. In the chapter called "The Grand Miracle," Lewis, in his inimitable style, described the incarnation of Christ: "In the Christian story God descends to re-ascend. He comes down; down from the heights of absolute being into time and space, down into humanity . . . down to the very roots and sea-bed of the Nature He has created.

"But He goes down to come up again and bring the ruined world up with Him. One has the picture of a strong man stooping lower and lower to get himself underneath some great complicated burden. He must stoop in order to lift, he must almost disappear under the load before he incredibly straightens his back and marches off with the whole mass swaying on his shoulders.

"Or one may think of a diver, first reducing himself to nakedness, then glancing in mid-air, then gone with a splash, vanished, rushing down through green and warm water into black and cold water, down through increasing pressure into the death-like region of ooze and slime and old decay; then up again, back to colour and light, his lungs almost bursting, till suddenly he breaks surface again, holding in his hand the dripping, precious thing that he went down to recover. He and it are both coloured now that they have come up into the light: down below, where it lay colourless in the dark, he lost his colour, too" ([New York: Macmillan, 1960], pp. 111-12).

That was how Lewis approached the incarnation, the central miracle of Christianity, which is also addressed in Philippians 2:5-8. In those verses Jesus is shown to be the perfect model of humility—the perfect illustration of Paul's instructions in Philippians 2:3-4. He did nothing out of selfishness or conceit but regarded others as more important than Himself. Yet beyond the example of Christ are the theological implications of Christ's humiliation.

Lesson

I. CHRIST WAS GOD (v. 6a)

"[Christ] existed in the form of God."

A. The Existence of Christ

Paul began by affirming that Jesus is God. That is where the incarnation began and whence Christ began the descent of His humiliation. The Greek word translated "existed" (*huparchō*) is not the common verb for "being" (*eimi*). *Huparchō* stresses the essence of a person's nature—his continuous state or condition (cf. William Barclay, *The Letters to the Philippians, Colossians, and Thessalonians* [Philadelphia: Westminster, 1976], p. 35). It expresses what one is, unalterably and inalienably, by nature. Paul's point was that Jesus Christ is unalterably and continuously existing in the form of God.

B. The Essence of Christ

1. The interpretive issue

Clarifying the meaning of the Greek word translated "form" (*morphe*) is crucial to a proper understanding of this passage. In English we have used that word to make words such as *endomorph* and *ectomorph*. *Morphe* "always signifies a form which truly and fully expresses the being which underlies it" (James Hope Moulton and George Milligan, *The Vocabulary of the Greek Testament* [Grand Rapids: Eerdmans, 1930], p. 417). The word describes essential being or nature —in this case the essential being of God.

Morphe may be better understood when compared to the Greek word *schema*. Both words are translated in English as "form." Although that is the best English

9

translation for each term, the meaning of each is not properly represented unless a distinction is made between them.

Morphe expresses the essential character of something—what it is in and of itself. *Schema* emphasizes outward form, or appearance. *Morphe* expresses the unchangeable, whereas *schema* represents that which may change. For example, all men possess manhood. They possess manhood from the time they are conceived until they die. That is their *morphe*. But the essential character of manhood is shown in various *schema*. At one time a man is an embryo, then a baby, then a child, then a boy, then a youth, then a young man, then an adult, and finally an old man. The *morphe* of manhood remains the same, but the *schema* changes.

In using the word *morphe* in Philippians 2, Paul was saying Jesus possessed the unchangeable, essential nature of God. That interpretation of the first phrase of verse 6 is strengthened by the second phrase, which says Jesus was equal with God. Being in the form of God speaks of Christ's equality with God.

2. The scriptural support

The deity of Christ is the heart of the Christian faith. Inevitably when people attack the Christian faith, they attack the deity of Christ.

a) John 1:1—"In the beginning was the Word, and the Word was with God, and the Word was God." John, under the inspiration of the Holy Spirit, began his gospel by affirming the deity of Christ.

b) John 1:3-4—John further declared Christ's deity when he wrote, "All things came into being by [Christ], and apart from Him nothing came into being that has come into being. In Him was life; and the life was the light of men."

c) John 1:14—Christ "became flesh, and dwelt among us, and we beheld His glory, glory as of the only begotten from the Father."

d) John 8:58—Jesus said, "Before Abraham was born, I am." Jesus appropriated to Himself the name of God, who said, "I am who I am" (Ex. 3:14).

e) Colossians 1:15-17—Paul wrote of Christ, "He is the image of the invisible God, the first-born of all creation. For by Him all things were created, both in the heavens and on earth, visible and invisible, whether thrones or dominions or rulers or authorities—all things have been created by Him and for Him. And He is before all things, and in Him all things hold together." Christ is the Creator.

The New Testament gives many examples of His ability to create. He made fish and bread (Matt. 14:15-21), new legs (John 5:2-9), new eyes (Matt. 12:22), new ears (Mark 7:32-37), a new mouth (Matt. 9:32-34), and new internal organs to replace diseased ones (Mark 5:25-34)—all acts of creation. Because Christ is Creator, He is God.

f) Hebrews 1:3—"[Christ] is the radiance of [God's] glory and the exact representation of His nature." Christianity begins with the recognition that Jesus Christ is in essence the eternal God. The simple and profound truth is that God became man.

II. CHRIST DID NOT CLING TO HIS EQUALITY WITH GOD (v. 6b)

"[Christ] did not regard equality with God a thing to be grasped."

The Greek word translated "equality" (*isos*) describes things that are exactly equal in size, quantity, quality, character, and number. The English word *isomer* comes from it. Isomers are chemical molecules that differ in structure from each other

11

but are identical in atomic elements and weights. We could say their forms are different, whereas their essential character is the same. *Isomorph* (equal form), *isometric* (equal measures), and *isosceles triangle* (a triangle with two sides of equal measure) are all English terms that describe equality. Christ is equal to God, and He exists in the form of God. A literal rendering of the Greek text into English is: "He did not regard the being equal with God"—a tremendous affirmation of the divinity of Christ.

The first step in the humiliation of Christ was that He did not hold on to equality with God. Although He did not cling to that equality, there is no question that Jesus claimed it and that the people who heard Him knew He claimed it.

A. John 5:18—"The Jews were seeking all the more to kill [Christ], because He not only was breaking the Sabbath, but also was calling God His own Father, making Himself equal with God." Today some people want to deny that Jesus is equal to God. Yet at the time Christ lived even His worst enemies, the apostate religious leaders, knew what Jesus claimed about Himself.

B. John 10:33—When Christ asked the leaders why they wanted to stone Him, they answered, "For a good work we do not stone You, but for blasphemy; and because You, being a man, make Yourself out to be God." They knew what He claimed.

C. John 10:38—Jesus said to them, "If I do [the works of the Father], though you do not believe Me, believe the works, that you may know and understand that the Father is in Me, and I in the Father."

D. John 14:9—Jesus said to Philip, "He who has seen Me has seen the Father."

E. John 20:28—Thomas addressed Jesus as "My Lord and my God."

Though He had all the rights, privileges, and honors of Godhood, Christ didn't grasp them. The word translated "grasp" originally meant "robbery" or "a thing seized by robbery." It eventually came to mean anything clutched, embraced, held

12

tightly, clung to, or prized. Paul meant that though He was God, Christ refused to cling to His favored position with all its rights and honors. He was willing to give them up for a season.

The incredible message of Christianity is far different from the world's man-made religious systems. If you go to India you will see people trying to appease various gods so that the gods won't be angry with them. But Christianity says God looked down on wretched sinners who hated Him and willingly yielded His privileges to give Himself for their sake. The incarnation expresses the humility and unselfish nature of the Second Person of the Trinity.

III. CHRIST EMPTIED HIMSELF (v. 7a)

"But [Christ] emptied Himself."

Note the contrast between verses 6 and 7: Christ didn't think equality something to be grasped but instead emptied Himself. Paul used a contrasting connective to show that being equal with God didn't lead Christ to fill Himself up but instead to empty Himself.

The Greek verb translated "emptied" (*kenoō*) is where we get the theological term *kenosis:* the doctrine of Christ's self-emptying as a part of His incarnation. The verb expresses Christ's self-renunciation, His refusal to cling to His advantages and privileges as God. The God who has a right to everything and who is fully satisfied within Himself emptied Himself.

What did Christ empty Himself of?

A. He Remained God

Christ did not empty Himself of His deity. He coexists with the Father and the Spirit, and for Him to have become less than God would have meant the Trinity would have ceased to exist. Christ could not become less than who He truly is.

Christ didn't exchange deity for humanity. Only God can die and conquer death, create, perform miracles, and speak as Christ did. Christ retained His divine nature.

B. He Renounced His Privileges

1. Heavenly glory

However, our Lord did give up His heavenly glory. That's why in John 17:5 Jesus prays, "Glorify Thou Me together with Thyself, Father, with the glory which I had with Thee before the world was." Christ gave up the glory of a face-to-face relationship with God for the muck of this earth. He gave up the adoring presence of angels for the spittle of men. He gave up the shining brilliance of heaven's glories and emptied Himself.

Every now and then on earth the glory of Christ peeked through, such as on the Mount of Transfiguration (Luke 9:28-36). Man glimpsed Christ's glory in His miracles, attitude, and words, as well as at the cross, at His resurrection, and at His ascension. But Christ emptied Himself of the continuous outward manifestation and personal enjoyment of heavenly glory.

2. Independent authority

Christ emptied Himself of His independent authority. He completely submitted Himself to the will of the Father and learned to be a servant. Philippians 2:8 says He was obedient, and we see that illustrated when He said in the garden, "Not as I will, but as Thou wilt" (Matt. 26:39). "He learned obedience from the things which He suffered" (Heb. 5:8) and affirmed that He came to do His Father's will (John 5:30)—not His own.

3. Divine prerogatives

He set aside the prerogatives of His deity—the voluntary display of His attributes. He knew what was in man (John 2:25). He was omnipresent: though not physically present, He saw Nathaniel under a tree (John 1:45-49). He didn't give up His deity, but He did give up the free exercise of His attributes, limiting Himself to the point of saying that even He did not know the time of His second coming (Matt. 24:36).

4. Eternal riches

He gave up His personal riches. "Though He was rich, yet for [our] sake He became poor, that [we] through His poverty might become rich" (2 Cor. 8:9). Christ was poor in this world; He owned very little.

5. A favorable relationship

God "made Him who knew no sin to be sin on our behalf" (2 Cor. 5:21). As a result our Lord cried out on the cross, "My God, My God, why hast Thou forsaken Me?"

Though Christ renounced all those privileges, He never ceased to be God. At any moment He could have blasted His enemies off the face of the earth, but He didn't. He voluntarily emptied Himself.

IV. CHRIST BECAME A SERVANT (v. 7b)

"[Christ took] the form of a bond-servant."

A. A Servant by Nature

When Christ emptied Himself, He not only gave up His privileges but also became a servant. Paul used the Greek word *morphe* ("form") again to indicate that Christ's servanthood was not merely external (Gk., *schema*) but of His essence. It was not like a cloak that could be put on and taken off. Christ was truly a servant. The only other New Testament use of the word *morphe* is in Mark 16:12. There Jesus appears in a resurrection *morphe*—a form fully expressing the nature of a resurrection body. In Philippians 2, Christ is shown as a true bondservant, doing the will of the Father. He submitted to the Father and to the needs of men as well. Jesus was everything that Isaiah 52:13-14 depicted—a Messiah who was a servant.

B. A Servant by Position

As God, Christ owns everything. But when He came into this world He borrowed everything: a place to be born, a place to lay His head (many nights He slept on the Mount of Olives), a boat to cross the Sea of Galilee and to preach from, an animal to ride into the city when He was triumphantly welcomed as King of kings and Lord of lords, a room for the Passover, and a tomb to be buried in. The only person ever to live on this earth who had the right to all its pleasures wound up with nothing and became a servant. Although He was King of kings and Lord of lords, the rightful heir to David's throne and God in human flesh, He had no advantages or privileges in this world. He was given little but served everyone. That was the incredible destiny of whom it is written, "All things came into being by Him, and apart from Him nothing came into being that has come into being" (John 1:3).

V. CHRIST IDENTIFIED WITH SINNERS (v. 7c)

"[Christ was] made in the likeness of men."

The descent of Christ continues as we move through verse 7. He was given all the essential attributes of humanity. He was more than God in a body. He became the God-man, being fully God and fully man. Like a man, Jesus was born and increased in wisdom and physical maturity (Luke 2:52).

A. Colossians 1:22—Christ "has now reconciled you in His fleshly body through death." He had a body just as we do.

B. Galatians 4:4—"God sent forth His Son, born of a woman, born under the Law."

C. Hebrews 2:14—"Since . . . the children share in flesh and blood, He Himself likewise also partook of the same." Christ had the same flesh and blood that we have. When He came into the world, He came in normal human flesh that experienced all the effects of the Fall. He knew sorrow, suffering, pain, thirst, hunger, and death. He felt all effects of the Fall without ever knowing or experiencing the sin of the Fall.

D. Hebrews 2:17—Jesus "had to be made like His brethren in all things, that He might become a merciful and faithful

16

high priest." For Christ to feel what we feel, He needed to be made like us. He experienced all the tests and temptations we do but never gave in to sin. That's why He is such a faithful and understanding High Priest.

E. Hebrews 4:15—"We do not have a high priest who cannot sympathize with our weaknesses, but one who has been tempted in all things as we are, yet without sin."

VI. CHRIST LOOKED LIKE A MAN (v. 8a)

"[Christ was] found in appearance as a man."

At first glance that sounds like a repetition of the end of verse 7, "being made in the likeness of men." We could paraphrase verse 8 to read, "He was discovered to appear as a man." The difference between that and verse 7 is a shift in focus. Here we view the humiliation of Christ from the viewpoint of those who saw Him. Christ was the God-man, but as people looked at Him they saw the appearance (Gk., *schema*, "outward form") of a man. Paul was implying that though Christ appeared to be a man, there was much more to Him that could not naturally be seen.

For Christ to become man was humbling enough. For Him not to have been recognized must have been humiliating. He performed miracles and taught authoritatively, yet the typical responses were: "You are a Samaritan and have a demon" (John 8:48) and, "Is not this Jesus, the son of Joseph, whose father and mother we know? How does he now say, 'I have come down out of heaven'?" (John 6:42). Because their minds were darkened by sin, people recognized His humanity but could not see His deity. They could not recognize who He really was. They not only treated the King of kings as a man but as the worst of men—a criminal.

VII. CHRIST HUMBLED HIMSELF (v. 8b)

"[Christ] humbled Himself."

Instead of fighting back, Christ humbled Himself. If we had suffered as He did, we would have shouted, "That's enough!

I want My rights! Don't you know who I am?" We would have blasted everything to bits. But Christ humbled Himself.

Consider the trial of Christ. He said not a word to defend Himself throughout unbelievable humiliation. He defended Himself only by agreeing with His accusers' statements: "You have said it yourself" (Matt. 26:64). They mocked Him, punched Him, pulled out His beard, treated Him as scum—yet He did not say a word. He was silent and accepted man's abuse through each phase of His mock trial. He did not demand His rights but humbled Himself.

VIII. CHRIST WAS OBEDIENT TO THE POINT OF DEATH (v. 8c)

"[Christ was] obedient to the point of death."

At no time did our Lord say, "Stop! That's enough"—not in the middle of His trial, not when He was mocked, not when forced to walk half naked through the city of Jerusalem with a cross on His back, not even on the cross. Christ was obedient to the point of descending into the muck and slime of death that He might bring us out of death into life.

IX. CHRIST DIED ON A CROSS (v. 8d)

"[Christ faced] even death on a cross."

"Even" calls attention to the most shocking feature of Christ's humiliation. Christ suffered not just death but death on a cross—the most excruciating, embarrassing, degrading, painful, and cruel death ever devised. Crucifixion was originated by the Persians and adopted by the Romans. It was used to execute rebellious slaves and the worst of criminals. The Jewish people hated it because of Deuteronomy 21:23: "Anyone who is hung on a tree is under God's curse" (NIV*). Galatians 3:13 says, "Christ redeemed us from the curse of the Law, having become a curse for us—for it is written, 'Cursed is every one who hangs on a tree.'" The God who created the universe suffered the ultimate human degradation: hanging naked against the sky before a mocking world, with nails driven through His hands and feet.

* *New International Version.*

Conclusion

Somewhere along the path of Christ's descent you'd think He would have said to Himself, *These people really aren't worth redeeming. This is too degrading and humiliating!* But the grace and love of God toward sinners was such that Christ stooped to die for you and me. At the end of Paul's doctrinal survey of salvation in Romans, he said, "Oh, the depth of the riches both of the wisdom and knowledge of God! How unsearchable are His judgments and unfathomable His ways!" (11:33). He was in awe of God's plan of salvation—a plan no man would have devised.

If we had planned the incarnation, we probably would have wanted Christ to be born in a palace. His family would have been wealthy and prominent, and He would have been educated in the finest universities with elite teachers and the finest tutors. We would have orchestrated events so that everyone loved, revered, honored, and respected Him. He would have been in all the prominent places and met all the prominent people.

We would not have had Him born in a stable to a family in poverty. He would not have spent His youth in a carpenter's shop in an obscure town. Rather than a ragtag band of followers, we would have made sure He had only the best people as His disciples, and they would have had to pass stiff qualifying tests for the privilege.

We would not have allowed Him to be humiliated. We would have imprisoned or executed anyone who spit on Him, pulled His beard, mocked Him, or hurt Him. Our plan for the Messiah would have been very different from God's plan, and, as a result, no one could have been saved. It's no wonder the psalmist said, "Thy judgments are like a great deep" (Ps. 36:6). God's ways are unsearchable, His truths profound. And that divine purpose was accomplished in Christ on our behalf.

Focusing on the Facts

1. The perfect illustration of Paul's instructions in Philippians 2:3-4 was _____ (see p. 9).

2. In Philippians 2:6, Paul begins by affirming that Jesus Christ is
_____ (see p. 9).
3. What does the Greek word *morphe* mean? Why is that important (see p. 10)?
4. How do the Greek words *morphe* and *schema* differ in meaning (see p. 10)?
5. Is it important that Paul chose to use the Greek word *morphe* to describe Christ? Why or why not (see pp. 10-11)?
6. What does Colossians 1:15-17 say about Christ? What does that say about His deity (see p. 11)?
7. What does the Greek term *isos* in Philippians 2:6 tell us about Christ (see p. 12)?
8. What does the incarnation express about the Second Person of the Trinity (see p. 13)?
9. When Christ emptied Himself, did He stop being God? Why or why not (see p. 14)?
10. What did Christ give up when He emptied Himself (see pp. 14-15)?
11. When Christ emptied Himself, what did He take on (Phil. 2:7; see p. 16)?
12. Was Jesus Christ truly a man? Why or why not (see p. 17)?
13. By using the Greek word *schema* in verse 8, what is Paul implying about Christ (see p. 18)?
14. Why couldn't those who knew Jesus see that He was God (see p. 18)?
15. How far did the humility and obedience of Christ extend (Phil. 2:8; see pp. 18-19)?

Pondering the Principles

1. It can be easy to let the great theological truths of Philippians 2:5-8 obscure the practical intent of its context. Those truths are but an illustration of the humble attitude that is to characterize every believer (see v. 5). The Puritan Thomas Watson observed, "Love is a humble grace; it does not walk abroad in state; it will creep upon its hands; it will stoop and submit to anything whereby it may be serviceable to Christ" (*All Things for Good* [Edinburgh: Banner of Truth Trust, 1986 reprint], p. 87). The love of Christ was such that He humbled Himself enough to die on a cross—an excruciating obedience that brought salvation to

mankind. Consider whether you are willing to humble yourself for the sake of Christ and others.

2. In Philippians 2:5-8 we see how the Savior lived and died for the glory of God. The early nineteenth-century American preacher Gardiner Spring wrote, "The cross is the emblem of peace, but it is also an emblem of ignominy and suffering: it was so to the Saviour—it is so to his followers; nor do they refuse any of its forms of reproach and suffering, but willingly endure them for the name of Christ" (*The Attraction of the Cross* [Edinburgh: Banner of Truth Trust, 1983 reprint], p. 192). Christ said that those who come after Him must take up their cross and follow Him (Matt. 16:24). In agreement with the example of Christ, have you taken up the cross of living for His honor and glory, no matter what?

2
Jesus' Death Shows Us How to Live

Outline

Introduction

Lesson
 I. The First Saying—Forgive Others (Luke 23:34)
    A. Christ's Example
    B. Man's Need
    C. The Christian's Response
 II. The Second Saying—Reach Out to Others (Luke 23:43)
    A. Christ's Example
    B. Man's Need
    C. The Christian's Response
 III. The Third Saying—Meet the Needs of Others (John 19:26-27)
    A. Christ's Example
    B. Mary's Need
    C. The Christian's Response
 IV. The Fourth Saying—Realize the Seriousness of Sin
    (Matt. 27:46)
    A. Christ's Example
    B. Man's Need
    C. The Christian's Response
 V. The Fifth Saying—Depend on Others (John 19:28)
 VI. The Sixth Saying—Finish What You Start (John 19:30)
 VII. The Seventh Saying—Commit Yourself to God (Luke 23:46)
    A. Christ's Example
    B. The Christian's Response

Conclusion
    A. Christ's Example
    B. Man's Need
    C. The Christian's Response

Introduction

First Peter 2:21 says, "You have been called for this purpose, since Christ also suffered for you, leaving you an example for you to follow in His steps." His suffering and humiliation were for a vital reason.

The life of Christ is an example for Christians to follow. The Bible tells us He was the perfect man—born without sin, committing no sin, holy, innocent, and undefiled. He is our perfect example. We are to be holy as He was holy, pure as He was pure, gentle as He was gentle, wise as He was wise, and humble as He was humble. Christ was obedient to God, and we are to imitate His example. Our service should be like His, and our attitude toward the world should reflect His attitude toward it.

First Peter 2:21 says that Christ is our example not only in His life but also in His death. Often we learn more about the character of a person by how he dies than by how he lives.

The truest revelation of ourselves generally comes in the time of deepest trial. Trial reveals character; adversity reveals virtue—or the lack thereof. Generally, the greater the trouble, the purer the revelation is of what we truly are. I don't think I really know a person if I've known him or her only during good times. It is the trying circumstances that reveal character. And we find that Jesus, at the time of His greatest trial—in His dying moments—was as holy as He was during His life.

In His death Jesus taught us how to live. We often look at His dying moments and observe that His death illustrates the seriousness of sin and the need for a Savior to pay the price for our iniquity. We recognize that by His substitutionary death, He died in our place. But Peter said that there's even more to the cross than that. Christ died for us, but He also died as an example to us. He died to show us how to live.

Christ revealed His character by what He said as He was dying. It could not be revealed by what He did—He was nailed to a cross and unable to do anything. From the earliest years the church has celebrated the death and resurrection of Christ by remembering His last seven sayings on the cross. They are actually principles for living.

Lesson

I. THE FIRST SAYING—FORGIVE OTHERS (Luke 23:34)

"Father, forgive them; for they do not know what they are doing."

A. Christ's Example

Christ died forgiving those who had sinned against Him. That is a principle by which we should live. Jesus had a forgiving heart even after a lifetime of experiencing mankind's worst treatment. Christ made the world and came into it, but the world would not acknowledge Him. Eyes blinded by sin did not want Him and refused to see beauty in Him. His birth in a stable foreshadowed the treatment He would receive from mankind throughout His life. Shortly after Christ's birth, King Herod tried to have Him killed, which was only the beginning of mankind's hostility toward Him. The cross was the climax of a lifetime of persecution.

Christ forgave His executioners after His mock trial of trumped-up accusations. The judge admitted that he found no fault in Him but used Him to appease a clamoring mob. Because no ordinary death would satisfy the implacable foes of Jesus, they made certain that He died the most painful and shameful death imaginable.

His forgiveness came as He hung on the cross, the victim (from a human perspective) of the hatred, animosity, bitterness, vengeance, and vile wickedness of men and demons. We would naturally have expected Him to cry out to God for pity or to shake His fist in the face of God for His unfair execution. If we had written the story, we might have shown Him crying maledictions and threats of vengeance upon His killers. But the Son of God did none of that. Instead, He asked God to forgive those who were taking His life.

Jesus understood the wretchedness of the human heart: "They do not know what they are doing." He was painfully aware of the ignorance of depravity. He knew His executioners understood neither the identity of their victim nor the enormity of their crime. They did not know they were killing the Prince of Life, their Creator. They did not know they were slaughtering the Messiah.

B. Man's Need

Christ's executioners needed forgiveness. The only way they could be ushered into the presence of a holy God was if their sins were forgiven. Christ prayed for the most profound need of His killers. He was more concerned that His wicked murderers be forgiven than that He be avenged. While "being reviled, He did not revile in return; while suffering, He uttered no threats, but kept entrusting Himself to Him who judges righteously" (1 Pet. 2:23).

Forgiveness is man's greatest need. It is the only way we can enter into fellowship with God and avoid hell, and that's why Jesus prayed for it. We need to recognize that apart from Christ we are sinners, unfit for the presence of a holy God. Noble ideals, good resolutions, and excellent rules to live by are useless if sin isn't dealt with. It would be the same as fitting shoes to paralyzed feet or buying glasses for blind eyes.

Jesus understood man's deep need. It did not matter to Him that the sin for which He sought forgiveness was the sin of His murder.

C. The Christian's Response

Christians are to be more concerned with God's forgiving those who sin against them than with vengeance. Stephen, while being stoned to death for preaching about Christ, prayed, "Lord, do not hold this sin against them!" (Acts 7:60). He followed the Lord's own example, and so should we.

II. THE SECOND SAYING—REACH OUT TO OTHERS (Luke 23:43)

"Truly I say to you, today you shall be with Me in Paradise."

A. Christ's Example

Two thieves were crucified with Christ—one on His right and the other on His left. In response to the request of one thief—"Jesus, remember me when You come in Your kingdom!"—Jesus replied, "Today you shall be with Me in Paradise" (Luke 23:42-43). Our Lord died bringing the truth of eternal life to a damned soul.

It is difficult to understand how Christ, hanging on a cross, feeling the venomous hate of His persecutors and, bearing the punishment of sinners throughout all ages, could at the same time be immediately concerned with the salvation of one of those sinners. But He was. Christ was never too preoccupied to be interested in leading someone to salvation. His life's commitment was to bring men and women to God.

B. Man's Need

The conversion of that thief is both remarkable and dramatic. At that moment, what was so convincing about Jesus? As yet there had been no outward sign that He was the Christ of God, Savior of the world, and the coming King. From a human standpoint He was but a victim. He was dying because He had been totally rejected. At the time of the thief's conversion no one was saying, "Behold, the Lamb of God who takes away the sin of the world!" (John 1:29). None affirmed that Jesus was the Son of God—even His friends had forsaken Him. He was weak, disgraced, and in a position of extreme shame. His crucifixion would have been considered totally inconsistent with anything related to the prophesied Messiah. The earth had not yet quaked (Matt. 27:51), the darkness had not yet come (Mark 15:33), graves had not yet been opened (Matt. 27:52), and the centurion had not yet said, "Truly this was the Son of God!" (Matt. 27:54).

In spite of these unfavorable and unconvincing circumstances, the thief was convinced that Jesus Christ was the Savior. Although at first he joined his companion in mocking Christ (Matt. 27:38, 44), he obviously had a change of heart and finally rebuked the other thief by affirming

Christ's sinlessness (Luke 23:40-41). In asking Jesus to remember him, he was pleading for forgiveness. He understood Christ's sinlessness and His identity as Savior. His request that Jesus remember him when entering into His kingdom shows that the thief believed in Christ's resurrection and second coming—he knew that death wasn't the end. The request also indicates that he understood Christ's sovereignty. All that was affirmed under the most unlikely of circumstances.

How was it possible for the thief to come to Christ under those conditions? There is perhaps no clearer illustration that salvation is not the work of man but the sovereign work of God. God, not circumstance, moved the thief's heart to understand the truth about Jesus Christ. Too often professing Christians seek to account for salvation by human cleverness and influence or by pointing to favorable circumstances, rather than attributing it to the matchless grace of God. Some think salvation happens because the preacher speaks well or because someone prays sincerely. Although salvation may indirectly result from those factors, it is the direct result of God's intervening grace.

C. The Christian's Response

Christ's desire for the salvation of sinners was constant. He came to seek and save the lost (Luke 19:10). Paul wrote that "Christ Jesus came into the world to save sinners" (1 Tim. 1:15). He accomplished that even while dying on a cross. He is our example for reaching out to others with the truth of the gospel.

III. THE THIRD SAYING—MEET THE NEEDS OF OTHERS (John 19:26-27)

"Woman, behold, your son . . . [Son,] behold, your mother!"

A. Christ's Example

Jesus died expressing selfless love. Standing at the foot of His cross stood a group of five people far different from the mocking crowd. With the apostle John was Mary, the mother of our Lord, who was experiencing the full force of Simeon's prophecy many years earlier that her soul would be pierced because of Jesus (Luke 2:34-35). Bound by love to her son's cross, she stood suffering in silence. Beside her stood Salome—possibly her sister—the mother of James and John. There was also Mary the wife of Clopas and Mary Magdalene out of whom Jesus had cast demons (Mark 15:40; Luke 8:2-3; John 19:25). It is fitting that the name *Mary* means "bitterness" in Hebrew.

The Romans crucified people close to the ground, so it is reasonable to assume that John and the women could have touched Him—perhaps they did. They were able to get near enough to hear Him speak softly. When Jesus said, "Woman, behold, your son," He didn't call her "Mother" because that relationship was over. Similarly, when He began His ministry, He identified her as "woman" (at the wedding in Cana; John 2:4). At the cross she was reminded again that she needed to regard Jesus not as her son but as her Savior. Yet His intent was not to call attention to Himself but to commit His mother to the care of John and John to the care of His mother.

B. Mary's Need

As Christ hung dying, His mother was on His heart. Out of all the crowd at the foot of cross, Jesus' mother was perhaps the neediest of all. It is likely that Joseph had died by this time, or Jesus wouldn't have had to make such a commitment. And He couldn't commit her to His half-brothers since they didn't believe in Him (John 7:5). He would not have committed the care of His believing mother into the hands of His unbelieving relatives.

C. The Christian's Response

On the cross Christ experienced the weight of the world's sins, the agony of the cross, and the wrath of almighty God—a far greater internal pain than His external pain. Yet in the midst of His pain He showed compassion. His thoughts were directed toward another, a demonstration of the purity of His character. That's how we are to live—never so overwhelmed with our own pain that we lose sight of the needs of others.

IV. THE FOURTH SAYING—REALIZE THE SERIOUSNESS OF SIN (Matt. 27:46)

"My God, My God, why hast Thou forsaken Me?"

A. Christ's Example

Jesus understood the seriousness of sin. Sin separates from God. *Forsaken* is one of the most painful words that a person could use to describe himself; it means alone and desolate. Jesus was forsaken. His cry meant, "My God, My God, with whom I have had eternal, unbroken fellowship, why have You deserted Me?" Against that backdrop of eternal intimacy, Christ's forsakenness has profound significance. Sin did what nothing else in the universe could do. Men couldn't separate the Father from the Son; demons couldn't; Satan couldn't. But sin caused the Son to suffer the most devastating state in the universe—separation from God.

B. Man's Need

God is too holy to look on sin (Hab. 1:13). As a result, sin alienates man from God. When Christ bore our sin on the cross, He reached the climax of His suffering. The soldiers had mocked Him, crushed a crown of thorns upon His head, scourged Him, struck Him, spit in His face, and pulled out the hairs of His beard. Even when suffering pain beyond description—His hands and feet pierced—He endured the cross and its shame in silence. Though taunted by the vulgar crowd and cursed by those crucified beside Him, He did not answer back. But when God forsook Him, Christ experienced a pain beyond all that, and He cried out in agony.

C. The Christian's Response

No earthly struggle, trial, or trouble should cause as much distress in us as our own sin. Like Christ, believers are to be profoundly anguished by the separation caused by sin. Jesus personally experienced the searing pain sin brings because it separated Him from the Father. We must understand the implication of our sin: it wrenches us away from God.

V. THE FIFTH SAYING—DEPEND ON OTHERS (John 19:28)

"I am thirsty."

Christ experienced the conditions of true humanity. He needed a drink, and He couldn't get it for Himself. Jesus depended on others, and we need to do the same.

Because Christ is familiar with human need He is a sympathetic High Priest (Heb. 2:17-18). The New Testament affirms that Christ was fully man—thirsty, weary, hungry, sleepy, happy, grieved. Christ depended on others to meet His needs. Sometimes those needs were met by Mary and Martha, sometimes by His mother. Like Jesus, we must be willing to show our frailties and learn to live dependently.

VI. THE SIXTH SAYING—FINISH WHAT YOU START (John 19:30)

"It is finished!"

"It is finished" (Gk., *tetelestai*) is a triumphant pronouncement. Christ died completing the work God gave Him to do.

It is one thing to end your life and yet another to finish it. To say your life is over may mean something far different than to say your work is done. I saw that principle in operation during the Los Angeles Marathon: everyone started and everyone stopped, but not everyone finished.

When most people's lives are over, their work is not done. When Jesus said, "It is finished," He meant He had finished His redeeming work. He came into this world "to put away sin by the sacrifice of Himself" (Heb. 9:26), and He did just that. He bore our sins in His own body and dealt Satan a blow to the head (Gen. 3:15). Just as Christ finished perfectly what God gave Him to do, so are we to finish our work. We must be more concerned with the work God has called us to do than the pain that work may cause us. Jesus endured the pain because He could see the end result (Heb. 12:2). That should be our motivation as well.

Paul faithfully followed Jesus' example. Therefore at the end of his life he could say, "I have finished the course" (2 Tim.

4:7). Yet in the same statement Paul affirmed that it hadn't been easy: he had had to fight to finish. That is how we are to live. Don't just live your life until it ends; live to finish the work God has given you to do.

VII. THE SEVENTH SAYING—COMMIT YOURSELF TO GOD (Luke 23:46)

"Father, into Thy hands I commit My spirit."

A. Christ's Example

Jesus died entrusting Himself to the promised care of God. We are to live the same way, casting all our anxieties upon God because He cares for us (1 Pet. 5:7). That means you must put your life, your death, and your destiny into His hands. That is what is meant by a life of faith: a life of complete trust in God.

God promised to raise Christ from the grave (Ps. 16:10). Jesus knew that promise because He often affirmed that He would suffer and die but would also rise again (Matt. 16:21; 26:32; Mark 9:9, 31; John 2:19). Based on God's promise He committed Himself to God's care. That's the only way to live—committing your life to God. "In all your ways acknowledge Him, and He will make your paths straight" (Prov. 3:6).

B. The Christian's Response

We are to live totally committed to God. Romans 12:1 says we are to present ourselves to God as living sacrifices. That means all that we are is His, and we trust Him for the outcome. First Peter 2:23 says Jesus "kept entrusting Himself to Him who judges righteously." He gave Himself to God regardless of the pain, the hostility, or the difficulty of the task. He knew God would do what was right, judge righteously, and bring to pass what He had promised. He was willing to face death and hell (1 Pet. 2:3) because He knew God would not fail Him. That's the kind of confidence we are to have.

Conclusion

A. Christ's Example

The Lord Jesus Christ lived a perfect life and died a perfect death. Both are a supreme example to us. His last words summed up the greatest elements of life: we are to forgive those who sin against us, present the saving truth to damned souls, love selflessly and show compassion to others, understand the serious implications of sin, admit our weakness and allow others to meet our needs, finish the work God gives us to do, and rest assuredly in the hands of a caring God, whose promises are sure.

B. Man's Need

As a result of Christ's perfect life and death, God raised Him from the dead. Then He set Him at His right hand in glory. That was God's affirmation of the perfect Person and work of His Son, and He affirms that He will also raise up those who are perfect.

If we are honest with ourselves, that doesn't necessarily sound like good news. We aren't always faithful evangelists. We are often insensitive to the pain and needs of others, and we act naively regarding sin's destructive power. Pride keeps us from living dependently. Laziness keeps us from finishing God's work. We often find ourselves trusting only what we can see. So we know we are imperfect, and it is mankind's failure to live perfectly that makes all mankind fit for hell.

What hope can we have then? Hebrews 10:14 says, "By one offering [Jesus Christ] has perfected for all time those who are sanctified." Christ was the only perfect man. God has graciously provided that we may be given the perfection of Christ, and through Him we may approach God in perfection.

Christians often say they are in Christ because they understand that if they weren't in Him, God wouldn't raise them to glory. His perfection becomes ours when we receive Him as Savior—His righteousness clothes us, and His perfection hides us. Because of our identity with Christ, God will raise us to glory and seat us on the throne with Christ. That is the gospel.

That doesn't mean Christians are perfect in this life. We still struggle with sin in this life, but we look forward to perfection in heaven. In the meantime we are covered by Christ's perfection and are progressively conformed to His image (2 Cor. 3:18).

C. The Christian's Response

Because Christ has covered us with His perfection, we ought to do all we can to live as perfectly as possible—to forgive, evangelize, and love as He did. Our desire to be free from sin should be as great as His was. We should depend on others, finish our appointed work, and totally trust God as He did. We will not earn perfection by doing that, but we will live up to the perfection we received from Christ when we received Him as Savior.

Focusing on the Facts

1. According to Peter, Christ is our example not only in the way He lived, but also in His _____ (see p. 24).
2. For Christ, the cross was the climax of a lifetime of _____ (see p. 25).
3. What is man's greatest need (see p. 26)?
4. Christ was never too preoccupied to be interested in leading someone to _____ (see p. 27).
5. At the time of the conversion of the thief on the cross, what circumstances existed to convince him that Jesus was the Son of God? Explain (see pp. 27-28).
6. The conversion of the thief shows that salvation is not a work of _____ but the sovereign work of _____ (see p. 28).
7. On the cross Mary was reminded that she needed to understand Jesus not as her son but as her _____ (see p. 29).
8. Describe the compassion of Christ on the cross for Mary. How does that apply to us (see p. 29)?

9. When Jesus cried, "My God, My God, why hast Thou forsaken Me," what did He mean (see p. 30)?
10. What separated the Father from the Son (see p. 30)?
11. How did Jesus depend on others (see p. 31)?
12. What did Jesus mean when He said, "It is finished" (see p. 31)?
13. In His death how did Jesus demonstrate a life of faith (see p. 32)?
14. What hope does mankind have in light of the perfection God requires (see pp. 33-34)?

Pondering the Principles

1. Today we are often told that the example of Christ need not be lived out in the life of believers. It is said that the burdens of the cross are only for those who desire deeper spiritual service. But Christ was emphatic: "Anyone who does not take his cross and follow me is not worthy of me" (Matt. 10:38, NIV). Consider the self-denial of the cross in your life: Are you willing to arise earlier to spend time with Christ (and lose some sleep)? Are you willing to be bold to proclaim Christ (and lose some popularity)? Are you willing to present the claims of Christ to someone you love dearly (and lose that person's affection)? The example of Christ claims no less for those who claim Him.

2. Christ's greatest humiliation is what a Christian glories in most. Paul said, "May I never boast except in the cross of our Lord Jesus Christ, through which the world has been crucified to me, and I to the world" (Gal. 6:14, NIV). British pastor Charles Haddon Spurgeon echoed Paul's thought in this way: "Look upon human glory as a thing that is tarnished, no longer golden; but corroded, because it came not to your Lord" (*The Treasury of the Bible*, vol. 3 [Edinburgh: Marshall, Morgan and Scott, 1962], p. 474). Often what the world glories in is retaliation (not forgiveness), tolerance (not evangelism), and selfishness (not selfless love). It glories in sin, denies that God has a claim on the world's obedience, and refuses to trust Him (if it acknowledges Him at all). What has the example of Christ on the cross taught you about the attitude you should adopt toward the things the world glories in?

3
The Exaltation of Christ—Part 1

Outline

Introduction
A. The Great Theme of the Passage
B. The Purpose of the Passage
C. The Promise of the Passage

Lesson
 I. The Source of Christ's Exaltation
A. The Basis of His Exaltation
B. The Elements of His Exaltation
C. The Meaning of His Exaltation
D. The Privileges of His Exaltation
E. The Reason for His Exaltation
II. The Title of Christ's Exaltation
A. The Significance of His New Name
B. The Authority of His New Name
C. The Foreshadowing of His New Name
D. The Reality of His New Name
E. The Implication of His New Name
F. The Testimonies to His New Name
G. The Sovereignty of His New Name
H. The Meaning of His New Name

Conclusion

Introduction

Philippians 2:9-11 says, "Therefore also God highly exalted Him, and bestowed on Him the name which is above every name, that at the name of Jesus every knee should bow, of those who are in heaven, and on earth, and under the earth, and that every tongue should confess that Jesus Christ is Lord, to the glory of God the Father."

A. The Great Theme of the Passage

In Philippians 2 Paul takes us from the humiliation of Christ (vv. 5-8; see pp. 8-20) to the exaltation of Christ (vv. 9-11). It is likely that verses 6-11 were a hymn of the early church. Those verses contain the great theme of the Christian faith: the humiliation (vv. 6-8) and exaltation (vv. 9-11) of Christ. As in this passage from Paul, Peter affirmed that the great theme of Old Testament prophecy was the sufferings of Christ and the glory to follow (1 Pet. 1:11). Regarding Christ, the writer of Hebrews says that "for the joy set before Him [He] endured the cross, despising the shame, and has sat down at the right hand of the throne of God" (Heb. 12:2). Christ understood His sufferings in light of His exaltation.

B. The Purpose of the Passage

Paul's purpose in Philippians 2 was not simply to detail the humiliation and exaltation of Christ but to use those truths as a practical illustration. Paul began his illustration with the words "Have this attitude in yourselves which was also in Christ Jesus" (v. 5).

The main idea in this section of Philippians is unity. In verses 2-4 Paul calls for unity produced by humility. In verses 5-11 we see Christ as the preeminent example of humility. But beyond the humiliation of Christ, Paul also affirms that He was exalted. The implication is that when we willingly humble ourselves as Christ did, God will lift us up.

That principle was not taught exclusively by Paul.

1. Matthew 23:12—Jesus said, "Whoever exalts himself shall be humbled; and whoever humbles himself shall be exalted." Humility and exaltation are reciprocal—if you exalt yourself, God will humble you; if you humble yourself, God will exalt you. Exaltation is the promised reward for faithful humility.

2. Luke 14:11—"Everyone who exalts himself shall be humbled, and he who humbles himself shall be exalted."

3. Luke 18:14—Jesus, contrasting a proud Pharisee with a humble tax collector, said, "Everyone who exalts himself shall be humbled, but he who humbles himself shall be exalted."

4. James 4:10—"Humble yourselves in the presence of the Lord, and He will exalt you."

5. 1 Peter 5:6—"Humble yourselves, therefore, under the mighty hand of God, that He may exalt you at the proper time."

It is true that the man who humbles himself is the one whom God exalts; the man who exalts himself is the one whom God will humiliate. In the divine economy it is by giving that one receives, by serving that one is served, by losing one's life that one finds life, and by dying to self that one lives. The one follows the other as surely as night follows day.

C. The Promise of the Passage

Jesus is an example of the exaltation that God will grant to every humble believer. When God said through the apostle Paul, "Let each of you regard one another as more important than himself" (Phil. 2:3), it was not without promise. The promise is seen in the illustration Paul used: Jesus Christ. Christ humbled Himself, and the Father wonderfully exalted Him.

Lesson

I. THE SOURCE OF CHRIST'S EXALTATION

A. The Basis of His Exaltation

The source of Christ's exaltation was God (v. 9). Whatever Christ was given came from God. The word translated "bestowed" (Gk., *charizomai*) means "gifted." God exalted and gifted Him. The word *therefore* at the beginning of verse 9 connects it to verses 5-8. It was because of Christ's humiliation that God exalted Him—the two are inseparable.

God "highly exalted" Christ (v. 9). The Greek preposition *huper* is used here as a prefix. We get the English words *hyper* and *super* from it. In a moment of redemptive history God highly exalted Christ.

B. The Elements of His Exaltation

Peter said Jesus was "raised up again" and "exalted to the right hand of God" (Acts 2:32-33). The exaltation of Christ includes both His resurrection and His coronation—His exaltation to the right hand of God. Peter and the apostles said, "The God of our fathers raised up Jesus. . . . He is the one whom God exalted to His right hand as a Prince and a Savior, to grant repentance to Israel, and forgiveness of sins" (Acts 5:30-31). Both the resurrection and coronation of Christ are affirmed, as well as the forgiveness of sins that comes with Christ's intercession for His people.

Ephesians 1:20 affirms both the resurrection ("He raised Him from the dead") and the coronation ("[He] seated Him at His right hand in the heavenly places"). Paul described Christ's coronation as one "far above all rule and authority and power and dominion, and every name that is named, not only in this age, but also in the one to come" (v. 21). The final element is described in Hebrews 4:14: "We have a great high priest who has passed through the heavens, Jesus the Son of God." That alludes to the ascension of Christ.

Christ's exaltation was thus fourfold: resurrection, ascension, coronation, and intercession. He rose from the dead and ascended into heaven. There He was seated on the throne of God to intercede as High Priest of His people. He sympathizes with us (Heb. 4:15); He is "holy, innocent, undefiled, separated from sinners and exalted above the heavens" (Heb. 7:26); and He "always lives to make intercession for [believers]" (Heb. 7:25). Just as the descent of Christ into humiliation occurred in stages (He was in the form of God but willingly gave that up; humbled Himself; became a servant; was made in the likeness of men; was found in fashion as a man; and was obedient to the point of death, even death on a cross [Phil. 2:5-8; see pp. 8-20]), so His resurrection, ascension, coronation, and intercession show the stages of His exaltation by God.

We Will Be Like Him

All believers will follow Christ in His exaltation. We will experience resurrection. We will also ascend—not only the believers at the time of the rapture but all believers. When in heaven we will experience coronation, for we will sit with Christ on His throne. We will no longer need our Lord's intercessory ministry, for the work of transformation will be complete. The path of glory Jesus followed beginning with His resurrection is the path we will follow as well. That is God's promise.

C. The Meaning of His Exaltation

A question that often springs to mind regarding the exaltation of Christ is how Jesus could be exalted since He is already God. We find the answer in Jesus' high priestly prayer in John 17, where He asked the Father to restore to Him the glory He had with the Father before the world began (v. 5). Christ's request shows that He gave up something that God would give back to Him. Christ gave up His glory in the incarnation. Beyond glorification, in His exaltation Christ would receive more than He had before.

How is that possible? God has it all. Christ didn't become any more God or any more perfect; He was already the most high God—King of kings and Lord of lords. But as the God-Man, a new state of being for Him, He suffered things and was given things He would not otherwise have had if He

41

had not become the God-Man. For example, He would never have had the privilege of being the interceding High Priest of His people if He had never been touched with the feelings of their infirmities—tempted in all points like them. If He had not become the God-Man, He would never have become the substitute for our sin by bearing our sins in His own body on the cross. As God He was incapable of elevation, but as the God-Man He could be lifted from the lowest degradation to the highest degree of glory. So in a sense He received from the Father privileges He didn't have before—privileges He gained because of His incarnation.

Jesus "was declared to be the Son of God with power by the resurrection from the dead" (Rom. 1:4). At His ascension He was surrounded by myriads of holy angels and was seated at the Father's right hand. He was elevated to that position as the God-Man—a state of being that was His only because of His incarnation. Thus He entered upon the rights and privileges not only of God as God but of God as the God-Man. His exaltation was not with regard to His nature or eternal place within the Trinity but with regard to His new character as the God-Man.

D. The Privileges of His Exaltation

When Jesus came into the world, He entered into a state of being He had never before experienced. His exaltation was the reversal of His humiliation—He who was poor became rich; He who was rejected became accepted; He who had learned obedience entered upon the administration of a power that calls all others to obey Him. Commentator William Hendricksen wrote, "As king, having by his death, resurrection, and ascension achieved and displayed his triumph over his enemies, he now holds in his hands the reigns of the universe, and rules all things in the interest of his church (Eph. 1:22-23). As prophet he through his Spirit leads his own in all the truth. And as priest (High-priest according to the order of Melchizedek) he, on the basis of his accomplished atonement, not only intercedes but actually lives forever to make intercession for those who draw near to God through him" (*Philippians, Colossians and Philemon* [Grand Rapids: Baker, 1962], p. 114). And God was the source of Jesus' exaltation.

1. Romans 14:9—"For this end Christ died and lived again, that He might be Lord both of the dead and of the living." Christ humbled Himself that God might exalt Him as Lord of all.

2. 1 Corinthians 15:24-25—Paul said that after all are made alive in Christ, "then comes the end, when He delivers up the kingdom to the God and Father, when He has abolished all rule and all authority and power. For He must reign until He has put all His enemies under His feet." Christ is now functioning under authority given Him by God. God exalted Him to the place where He is the sovereign of everything.

3. John 5:22—The Father "has given all judgment to the Son." That was God's gift to the Son, which was part of the Son's exaltation.

E. The Reason for His Exaltation

In Philippians 2:9 Paul says that God "bestowed on Him the name." The Greek word translated "bestowed" means "to give graciously" or "wholeheartedly." Christ so fully and completely accomplished God's plan of redemption that God wholeheartedly and graciously poured out on Christ the gifts of exaltation. Though He could not be made more than God, He now enjoys all the privileges of God as well as all the privileges of the God-Man that He now is.

II. THE TITLE OF CHRIST'S EXALTATION

A. The Significance of His New Name

The key point of Philippians 2:9-11 is the title of Christ's exaltation. Verse 9 says, "God highly exalted Him, and bestowed on Him the name which is above every name." Paul used the definite article before the word *name*. So the question arises, what is the name that is above every name? According to Hebrews 1:4, it is a more excellent name than the angels have. To be consistent with Scripture, it has to be a name that goes beyond merely distinguishing one person from another. It has to be a name that describes Christ's nature—revealing something of His inner being. Only such a name would cause Him to be clearly ranked above all others. Paul wasn't referring to a comparative name but a superlative name: one that would set Christ above and beyond all comparison.

Change of name in Scripture indicates the commencement of a unique relationship. When God established His covenant with Abram, He changed his name to "Abraham" (Gen. 17:5). When God entered into a unique relationship with Jacob He gave him the name "Israel" (Gen. 32:22-32). In the New Testament Jesus called a man named Simon to follow Him. Jesus gave him a new name: Peter (Matt. 16:18). To the churches at Pergamum and Philadelphia the Lord promised that those who overcame would receive a new name (Rev. 2:17; 3:12). Those names were given to mark a definite stage in a person's life. God has done that throughout redemptive history. Philippians 2:9 affirms that God gave Christ a name. He had had many names—Jesus, Christ, Son of Man, Son of God, Messiah—but He received a new name.

B. The Authority of His New Name

Some assume that the new name is Jesus because verse 10 says, "At the name of Jesus every knee should bow." But that wasn't a new name; it was bestowed at birth—"You shall call His name Jesus, for it is He who will save His people" (Matt. 1:21). Nor is the name Jesus above every other name. There have been a lot of people named Jesus. The only name mentioned in Philippians 2:9-11 that is above every name is *Lord*. In verse 11 Paul says, "Every tongue should confess that Jesus Christ is Lord." That is the only name God gave Christ that is above every name. Whoever is Lord is in control.

That name is a New Testament synonym for Old Testament descriptions of Yahweh (the Old Testament name of God), which show God as sovereign ruler. It signifies rulership based on power and authority. The gospels clearly show that Lord was to be His new name. Christ acknowledged before Pilate that He was a King (Mark 15:2; John 18:37). Thomas looked on the resurrected Christ and worshiped Him, saying, "My Lord and my God" (John 20:28). Though it was always evident that Christ was the living Lord, it was in His exaltation that He was formally given the name

Lord—a title that is His as the God-Man. On earth He was known by many names, but now He bears the name that is above every name: Lord.

Verse 10 says, "At the name of Jesus every knee should bow." Verse 11 continues that "every tongue should confess that Jesus Christ is Lord." Verse 10 doesn't say *at the name Jesus* every knee should bow, but at the name *of* Jesus every knee should bow. The name *of* Jesus immediately bestowed by the Father was Lord. It is not the name Jesus that makes people bow—that's the name of His incarnation—but the name *Lord*.

C. The Foreshadowing of His New Name

That the name mentioned in verse 9 is Lord is confirmed by Paul's allusion to Isaiah 45:21-23, which says, "Declare and set forth your case; indeed, let them consult together. Who has announced this from of old? Who has long since declared it? Is it not I, the Lord? And there is no other God beside Me, a righteous God and a Savior; there is none except Me. Turn to Me, and be saved, all the ends of the earth; for I am God, and there is no other. I have sworn by Myself, the word has gone forth from My mouth in righteousness and will not turn back, that to Me every knee will bow, every tongue will swear allegiance." God said through Isaiah that He is sovereign—the Lord of all. That is what Paul was referring to when He said that every knee would bow and every tongue confess (or admit) that Jesus Christ is Lord. Only God is Lord.

D. The Reality of His New Name

Is Jesus Christ Lord? According to the declaration of the Father He is. To be called Lord is to have a name above every other name. It means Jesus is the sovereign God. He is not only God according to His being, but God with all the attributes ascribed to God. Therefore He rules as sovereign.

E. The Implication of His New Name

Some say that all Paul meant was that Jesus is God, apart from exercising sovereignty. But once He is acknowledged as God He must be acknowledged as possessing the attribute of sovereignty. To say He is God is to affirm that He is in charge.

We cannot know Christ any other way than as Lord. That's why the first creed in the history of the church, given in verse 11, says, "Jesus Christ is Lord." Every Christian must acknowledge that. It is the bottom line of the Christian faith, the very substance of Christianity. We don't make Him Lord after salvation. Every time I hear someone say, "You need to make Jesus Lord" it is as repellant to me as hearing fingernails scraped down a blackboard. We never make Jesus Lord—God has already done that.

Puritan John Flavel put it this way: "The gospel offer of Christ includes all his offices, and gospel faith just so receives him; to submit to him, as well as to be redeemed by him; to imitate him in the holiness of his life, as well as to reap the purchases and fruits of his death. It must be an entire receiving of the Lord Jesus Christ" (*The Works of John Flavel*, vol. 2 [London: Banner of Truth Trust, reprint], p. 111).

A. W. Tozer said, "To urge men and women to believe in a divided Christ is bad teaching, for no one can receive half of Christ, or a third of Christ, or a quarter of the Person of Christ! We are not saved by believing in an office nor in a work" (*I Call It Heresy!* [Harrisburg, Pa.: Christian Publications, 1974], pp. 10-11). Jesus is Lord, and those who refuse Him as Lord cannot call Him Savior. Everyone who truly receives Him surrenders to His authority.

F. The Testimonies to His New Name

The truth that Jesus Christ is Lord rings throughout the New Testament.

1. Luke 2:11—"Today in the city of David there has been born for you a Savior, who is Christ the Lord." Even at His birth it was affirmed that Christ is Lord. That's who He is, and He rightfully bears that name. But it is a name that was bestowed by the Father when Christ's atoning work was done.

2. John 13:13—To the apostles Jesus said, "You call me Teacher and Lord; and you are right, for so I am."

46

3. Acts 2:36—On the day of Pentecost Peter preached, "Let all the house of Israel know for certain that God has made Him both Lord and Christ—this Jesus whom you crucified."

4. Acts 10:36—The message of God "sent to the sons of Israel . . . [was] peace through Jesus Christ (He is Lord of all)." To preach Christ is to preach Him as Lord. More than ninety times in the book of Acts Jesus is referred to as Lord.

5. Romans 10:9-13—Paul said, "If you confess with your mouth Jesus as Lord, and believe in your heart that God raised Him from the dead, you shall be saved; for with the heart man believes, resulting in righteousness, and with the mouth he confesses, resulting in salvation. For the Scripture says, 'Whoever believes in Him will not be disappointed.' For there is no distinction between Jew and Greek; for the same Lord is Lord of all."

6. Romans 14:11—"It is written, 'As I live, says the Lord, every knee shall bow to Me, and every tongue shall give praise to God.'" Who was Paul talking about? Verse 9 says, "Christ died and lived again, that He might be Lord both of the dead and of the living." Romans 14:9-11 quotes Isaiah 45:23, the same passage Paul used in Philippians 2. His emphasis is that Christ is Lord.

7. 1 Corinthians 8:6—"For us there is but one God, the Father, from whom are all things, and we exist for Him; and one Lord, Jesus Christ.

8. 1 Corinthians 12:3—"No one can say, 'Jesus is Lord,' except by the Holy Spirit." The Spirit's moving on the heart enables one to call Jesus Lord.

9. 1 Corinthians 15:57—Paul said, "Thanks be to God, who gives us the victory through our Lord Jesus Christ."

10. 2 Corinthians 4:5—According to Paul, "We do not preach ourselves but Christ Jesus as Lord."

11. Revelation 17:14; 19:16—Jesus is "Lord of lords and King of kings."

G. The Sovereignty of His New Name

Scripture never speaks of any human being's making Jesus Lord. It is God who made Him Lord (Acts 2:36). Yet we often read statements such as this: "It is imperative to trust Christ as personal Savior and be born again. But that is only the first decision. The decision to trust Christ as Savior and then make Him Lord are two separate and distinct decisions. The two decisions may be close or distant in time. Salvation must always precede lordship. But it is possible to be saved without ever making Christ Lord of your life." In effect that is to say Christ isn't Lord unless we give Him permission—a completely unbiblical assertion. To be saved you must confess Jesus as Lord.

Jesus is called Lord throughout the New Testament. To eliminate the lordship of Christ from invitations to salvation would result in the elimination of numerous passages of Scripture. Peter's sermon in Acts 2—"Everyone who calls on the name of the Lord shall be saved" (Acts 2:21)—would need to be modified. Paul and Silas's method of presenting the gospel—"Believe in the Lord Jesus Christ, and you shall be saved" (Acts 16:31)—would need to be corrected.

H. The Meaning of His New Name

The centrality of the lordship of Christ is clear in the New Testament gospel. The Jesus who is Savior cannot be separated from the Jesus who is Lord. God cannot be separated from His authority, dominion, rulership, and right to command. When we acknowledge that Jesus is God, we mean He is all that God is.

The Greek word translated "Lord" (*kurios*) primarily refers to the right to rule. Its inherent meaning is not deity but rulership. *Kurios* is thus used in the New Testament to describe a master or owner. It was a title of respect for anyone in control. It became the official title of the Roman emperors. They were called *kurios* in Greek and *dominus* in Latin, both signifying master or lord. It was used as a title for heathen deities. The translators of the Greek Old Testament used *kurios* to translate the name of God (the Hebrew word *Yahweh*). So although deity could be associated with the word, its primary meaning is rulership—secular or otherwise. To say Jesus is *kurios* certainly implies deity, but the main thought is authority. Regardless of the meaning taken—master, owner, ruler, leader, God—all acknowledge Jesus' authority over us.

Conclusion

That Jesus is Lord is at the heart of the gospel. The source of Christ's exaltation is God; the title of His exaltation is Lord. Paul said everyone is going to acknowledge the lordship of Christ sooner or later. It is my prayer that you acknowledge that He is Lord by choice and not by force.

Focusing on the Facts

1. Who or what was the source of Christ's exaltation (see p. 40)?
2. It was because of Christ's _____ that God exalted Him (see p. 40).
3. The elements of Christ's exaltation were fourfold: _____, _____, _____, and _____ (see p. 40).
4. Christ gave up His _____ in the incarnation (see p. 41).
5. Christ was exalted with regard to His new character as _____ _____ (see pp. 41-42).
6. Why did God wholeheartedly and graciously pour out upon Christ the gifts of exaltation (see p. 43)?
7. What is the key point of Philippians 2:9-11 (see p. 43)?
8. What does a change of name indicate in Scripture (see pp. 43-44)?
9. What is the only name mentioned in Philippians 2:9-11 that is a name above every name (see p. 44)?
10. What Old Testament passage shows us the name to which Paul referred in Philippians 2:9-11 (see p. 45)?
11. Jesus' new name means that He is the _____ (see p. 45).
12. What is the bottom line of the Christian faith (see pp. 45-46)?
13. Can those who refuse Jesus as Lord regard Him as Savior? Why or why not (see p. 46)?
14. What New Testament passages confirm that Jesus is Lord (see pp. 46-47)?

15. What is wrong with the statement "The decision to trust Christ as Savior and then make Him Lord are two separate distinct decisions" (see p. 48)?

16. If God the Father can't be separated from His authority, dominion, rulership, and right to command, can God the Son be separated from those qualities? Why or why not (see p. 48)?

17. What is the meaning of the Greek word *kurios* (see pp. 48-49)?

Pondering the Principles

1. The humiliation and exaltation of Christ are a lesson for all believers: "As Christ ceased not to be a King because He was a servant, nor to be a lion because he was like a lamb, nor to be God because He was made a man, nor to be a judge because He was judged; so a man does not lose his honour by humility, but he shall be honoured for his humility" (Henry Smith, cited in *A Puritan Golden Treasury* [Edinburgh: Banner of Truth Trust, 1977], p. 149). Does your life demonstrate a Christlike humility that God will delight to honor by exaltation?

2. The lordship of Jesus Christ is a crucial issue. Many in our day seem to believe that they can accept the work of Christ on the cross apart from worshiping Him as King. Nearly one hundred years ago Charles Haddon Spurgeon wrote, "I cannot conceive it possible for anyone truly to receive Christ as Saviour and yet not to receive him as Lord. One of the first instincts of a redeemed soul is to fall at the feet of the Saviour, and gratefully and adoringly to cry, 'Blessed Master, bought with thy precious blood, I own that I am thine—thine only, thine wholly, thine for ever. Lord, what wilt thou have me to do?' A man who is really saved by grace does not need to be told that he is under solemn obligations to serve Christ; the new life within him tells him that. Instead of regarding it as a burden, he gladly surrenders himself—body, soul, and spirit, to the Lord who has redeemed him, reckoning this to be his reasonable service" (*Metropolitan Tabernacle Pulpit*, vol. 56 [Pasadena, Tex.: Pilgrim Publications, 1979], p. 617). Take a moment now to acknowledge the lordship of Christ in your own life—it is only your reasonable service to do so.

4
The Exaltation of Christ—Part 2

Outline

Introduction

Review

I. The Source of Christ's Exaltation
   A. The Basis of His Exaltation
   B. The Elements of His Exaltation
      1. Resurrection
      2. Ascension
      3. Coronation
      4. Intercession
   C. The Meaning of His Exaltation
   D. The Privileges of His Exaltation
   E. The Reason for His Exaltation
II. The Title of Christ's Exaltation

Lesson

III. The Response to Christ's Exaltation
   A. Why Christ Is to Be Acknowledged
      1. Because it is God's will
      2. Because He is God
   B. Who Is to Acknowledge Christ
      1. Those in heaven
         a) The angels
         b) The redeemed
      2. Those on earth
         a) The obedient
         b) The disobedient
      3. Those under the earth
   C. What Is to Be Acknowledged

IV. The Purpose of Christ's Exaltation

Conclusion

Introduction

When you consider the humiliation of Christ—that He was despised, hated, rejected, ignored, cursed, spat on, slapped, beaten, punched, betrayed, denied, whipped, slandered, and finally crucified—if you love Christ, your heart should be pained. The cruel injustice, blatant hostility, and ingratitude that brought Him abuse will always be a source of grief to those who adore Him. Yet it was God's plan that He be humiliated. He who existed in the form of God "did not regard equality with God a thing to be grasped, but emptied Himself, taking the form of a bond-servant, and being made in the likeness of men. And being found in appearance as a man, He humbled Himself by becoming obedient to the point of death, even death on a cross" (Phil. 2:6-8).

Review

Verses 9-11 describe the Lord's return to the glory He now possesses with God: "God highly exalted Him, and bestowed on Him the name which is above every name, that at the name of Jesus every knee should bow, of those who are in heaven, and on earth, and under the earth, and that every tongue should confess that Jesus Christ is Lord, to the glory of God the Father."

The gospel is not complete without the exaltation of Jesus Christ. In this marvelous hymn of the early church we see our Lord descending from His glory to take the form of a servant and then ascending and returning to the glory He had with the Father before the world began. That is the complete Christian message. Too often we are content to leave Christ in His humiliation—hanging on a cross. We hide the fullness of the gospel when we do not properly proclaim His exaltation.

I. THE SOURCE OF CHRIST'S EXALTATION (see pp. 39-43)

The source of Christ's exaltation is indicated in verse 9: "God highly exalted Him, and bestowed on Him the name." Only God rightfully exalts anyone. When Christ was exalted by God, He was placed where He rightfully belonged.

A. The Basis of His Exaltation (see pp. 39-40)

B. The Elements of His Exaltation (see pp. 40-41)

In Philippians 2:6-8 we noted the steps of Christ's descent (see pp. 9-20). In verses 9-11 we see the steps of His ascent (see pp. 40-41).

1. Resurrection

God raised Christ from the dead. That was the first step from humiliation to exaltation. In Acts 13 Paul preached on the resurrection of Christ. He said, "[God] raised up Jesus, as it is also written in the second Psalm, 'Thou art My Son; today I have begotten Thee.' And as for the fact that He raised Him up from the dead, no more to return to decay, He has spoken in this way: 'I will give you the holy and sure blessings of David.' Therefore He also says in another Psalm, 'Thou wilt not allow Thy holy one to undergo decay.' For David, after he had served the purpose of God in His own generation, fell asleep, and was laid among his fathers, and underwent decay; but He whom God raised did not undergo decay. Therefore let it be known to you, brethren, that through Him forgiveness of sins is proclaimed to you, and through Him everyone who believes is freed from all things, from which you could not be freed through the law of Moses" (vv. 33-39). Christ's death and resurrection provided forgiveness and freedom from sin, the law, and death.

2. Ascension

Acts 1:9-11 records the second step in the exaltation of Christ. After Christ finished His final instructions to His disciples, "He was lifted up while they were looking on, and a cloud received Him out of their sight. And as they were gazing intently into the sky while He was departing, behold, two men in white clothing stood beside them; and they also said, 'Men of Galilee, why do you stand looking into the sky? This Jesus, who has been taken up from you into heaven, will come in just the same way as you have watched Him go into heaven.'" Acts 2:33 says that the result of His ascension was exaltation to the right hand of God. From that position He poured forth the Holy Spirit on the day of Pentecost.

3. Coronation

Matthew 28:18 records Jesus' affirmation of His authority: "All authority has been given to Me in heaven and on earth." Mark 16:19 says, "When the Lord Jesus had spoken to [the apostles], He was received up into heaven, and sat down at the right hand of God."

In Scripture the right hand is a symbol of power and authority. At the right hand of God Christ acts with the authority and the power of almighty God. Acts 7:55-56 records that as Stephen was stoned, he was full of the Holy Spirit and "gazed intently into heaven and saw the glory of God, and Jesus standing at the right hand of God; and he said, 'Behold, I see the heavens opened up and the Son of Man standing at the right hand of God.'"

What is the extent of Christ's authority?

a) Ephesians 1:20-22—"[God] seated Him at His right hand in the heavenly places, far above all rule and authority and power and dominion, and every name that is named, not only in this age, but also in the one to come. And He put all things in subjection under His feet, and gave Him as head over all things to the church."

b) Hebrews 2:9—"We do see Him who has been made for a little while lower than the angels, namely, Jesus, because of the suffering of death crowned with glory and honor." Christ is the sovereign of the universe. An understanding of Christ requires that we acknowledge Him not only as our humiliated Savior but also as our exalted Lord.

c) 1 Peter 3:22—"Angels and authorities and powers [have] been subjected to Him."

4. Intercession

The fourth phase of Christ's exaltation is His intercession for believers. He is in open session before the Father as the High Priest of His people. His first act was to send the Holy Spirit (Acts 2:33). Our sympathetic High Priest "has been tempted in all things as we are" (Heb. 4:15). "He is able to save forever those who draw near to God through Him, since He always lives to make intercession for [us]" (Heb. 7:25). Hebrews 4-9 is an extensive treatment of Christ's intercessory work. He grants us faith, repentance, and forgiveness.

In Hebrews 1 we see the resurrected, ascended, coronated, and interceding Christ in His majestic glory. He is heir of all things (v. 2). That is why He is entitled to the title deed to the earth, spoken of in Revelation 5:1-7. The deed was sealed seven times to make sure no one broke it open but the right person. The beginning of the book of Revelation shows Christ opening the title deed to the earth and taking possession of what is rightfully His as heir of all things.

Hebrews 1 further describes Christ as "the radiance of [God's] glory and the exact representation of [God's] nature. . . . When He had made purification of sins, He sat down at the right hand of the Majesty on high; having become as much better than the angels, as He has inherited a more excellent name than they. For to which of the angels did [God] ever say, 'Thou art My Son, today I have begotten Thee'? And again, 'I will be a Father to Him, and He shall be a Son to Me'? And when He again brings the firstborn into the world, He says, 'Let all the angels of God worship Him'" (vv. 3-7). Because Christ is the unique Son of God, the angels are called to worship Him.

The Father said of Christ, "Thy throne, O God, is forever and ever, and the righteous scepter is the scepter of His Kingdom. Thou hast loved righteousness and hated lawlessness; therefore God, Thy God, hath anointed Thee with the oil of gladness above Thy companions" (vv. 8-9). Christ is the eternal, righteous God. Only of Him can it be said, "Thou, Lord, in the beginning didst lay the foundation of the earth, and the heavens are the works of Thy hands" (v. 10). John said, "Apart from Him nothing came into being that has come into being" (John 1:3). Paul said, "From Him and through Him and to Him are all things" (Rom. 11:36). Hebrews 1:11-13 says, "'[The heavens and earth] will perish, but Thou remainest; and they all will become old as a garment, and as a mantle Thou wilt roll them up; as a garment they will also be changed. But Thou art the same, and Thy years will not come to an end.' But to which of the angels has He ever said, 'Sit at My right hand, until I make Thine enemies a footstool for Thy feet'?" Christ is superior to the angels. They are created beings who serve those who inherit salvation. So angels serve the redeemed, and both worship the exalted Lord Jesus Christ.

C. The Meaning of His Exaltation (see pp. 41-42)

D. The Privileges of His Exaltation (see pp. 42-43)

E. The Reason for His Exaltation (see p. 43)

The central truth of Christianity is that Jesus Christ is Lord. The gospel can't be understood apart from the lordship of Christ. He is to be confessed as Lord by the mouth and in the heart. Because Christ is the exalted Lord we have assurance that redemption is complete, our hope of heaven is secure, and we participate in the ongoing forgiveness belonging to those for whom He intercedes with the Father. A gospel that stops with the humiliation of Christ is incomplete. He must be seen as the resurrected, ascended, coronated, and interceding Lord. God's grace confers not only the gift of forgiveness that comes by faith but also the joy of willing submission by faith to the exalted Christ, who has purchased forgiveness. Both are essential in salvation (James 2:17-20; 1 John 1:6-7; 2:4-6). The proclamation of the gospel requires that we present both the humble Savior and the exalted Lord, who is one and the same person. Preaching half the gospel has produced people who believe that Jesus is only a humbled person who died to give them a free gift. They therefore have no sense of allegiance to His sovereign lordship.

II. THE TITLE OF CHRIST'S EXALTATION (see pp. 43-49)

The title of Christ's exaltation is Lord. Revelation 3:12 contains a beautiful promise given to the church at Philadelphia. Christ said He would write on those who overcome the name of God, the name of the city of God, and His own new name. That means if you're a believer, you're stamped with the name of God, heaven, and Christ's new name—*Lord*. That means you belong to God, heaven, and Jesus Christ the Lord. Revelation 19:16 says He will be called "King of kings, and Lord of lords."

Lesson

III. THE RESPONSE TO CHRIST'S EXALTATION

There's only one proper response to Christ's exaltation: "that at the name of Jesus every knee should bow, of those who are in heaven, and on earth, and under the earth, and that every tongue should confess that Jesus Christ is Lord" (Phil. 2:10-11). He deserves worship.

Verse 10 begins with the Greek word *hina* ("that"). *Hina* indicates purpose or result. We might translate the sentence, "He was given the name that is above every name in order that at the name of Jesus every knee will bow and every tongue confess that Jesus Christ is Lord." The reason Christ was given that name was to put Him in authority and cause everyone to bow to Him.

Is the Lordship of Christ Important?

According to Paul, the name of Jesus is Lord (Gk., *kurios*). At His name every knee will bow and every tongue confess. Christ died to accomplish our salvation in His humiliation. He was then resurrected, ascended, and coronated; and now He intercedes on our behalf. We are to know Christ as He is—as Lord—as well as by what He did for us on the cross. Salvation is for those who confess Jesus as Lord (Rom. 10:9-10). We see the same truth from a different perspective in Matthew 7:21-23. To those who falsely claim salvation by saying, "Lord, Lord," Christ will say, "I never knew you."

A. Why Christ Is to Be Acknowledged

1. Because it is God's will

It was God's expressed purpose that Christ's exaltation result in our worshiping Him. Philippians 2:10 says that at His name, Lord, we are to bow. The subjunctive mood here ("every knee should bow") implies that every knee will bow—either by choice or by force.

2. Because He is God

By God's grace some are enabled to acknowledge Christ's lordship by choice. Others will bow to Him because they are forced to do so. The phrases "every knee should bow" (v. 10) and "every tongue should confess" (v. 11) are taken from Isaiah 45:23, which strongly emphasizes the sole authority and sovereignty of God. In context the Lord said, "There is no other God besides Me, a righteous God and a Savior; there is none except Me. Turn to Me, be saved, all the ends of the earth; for I am God, and there is no other. I have sworn by Myself, the word has gone out of My mouth in righteousness and will not turn back, that to Me every knee will bow, every tongue will swear allegiance. They will say of Me, 'Only in the Lord are righteousness and strength'" (vv. 21-24). Isaiah spoke of the sovereignty and majesty of the Lord.

Isaiah 46:5-10 continues the thought: God said, "To whom would you liken Me, and make Me equal and compare Me, that we should be alike? Those who lavish gold from the purse and weigh silver on a scale hire a goldsmith, and he makes it into a god; they bow down, indeed they worship it. They lift it upon the shoulder and carry it; they set it in its place and it stands there. It does not move from its place. Though one may cry to it, it cannot answer; it cannot deliver him from his distress. Remember this, and be assured; recall it to mind, you transgressors. Remember the former things long past, for I am God, and there is no other; I am God, and there is no one like Me, declaring the end from the beginning and from ancient times things which have not been done, saying, 'My purpose will be established, and I will accomplish all My good pleasure.'"

Isaiah 45-46 clearly establishes that God is Lord and sovereign. He is in charge. In Philippians Paul says that the same that is true of God is true of the Lord Jesus Christ—every knee will bow and every tongue confess that He is Lord of all. We know Him as the Lord, and we know Him as Jesus—the names of His exaltation and humiliation. But He must be known as both in order to be known at all. One receives the gift of salvation by receiving both the humiliated Savior and by bowing the knee to a coronated, majestic, sovereign God.

B. Who Is to Acknowledge Christ

Philippians 2:10 affirms that the whole intelligent universe is called to worship Christ. Three categories are mentioned: "Those who are in heaven, and on earth, and under the earth." The King James Version says, "Of *things* in heaven, and *things* in earth, and *things* under the earth." The word *things* was added by the King James translators and for that reason appears in italics. But *things* don't worship; people and angels do. They are specified as those in heaven, on earth, and under the earth. The whole universe of intelligent beings will bow the knee and confess that Jesus Christ is Lord.

1. Those in heaven

Those in heaven consist of two groups: the angels and the spirits of redeemed believers (who await the resurrection of their bodies). Those who are in heaven already acknowledge that Jesus is Lord.

The angelic group consists of God's holy, elect angels—the unfallen seraphim, cherubim, and myriads of other angels who worship God in heaven. The spirits of redeemed believers are the triumphant saints now in the presence of Christ—"the general assembly and church of the first-born who are enrolled in heaven . . . the spirits of righteous men made perfect" (Heb. 12:23). Throughout their time in heaven they've been worshiping the Lord of glory.

a) The angels

Revelation 4 describes the worship of angels. In verses 2-3 we see God on His throne. Around the throne are twenty-four elders, before the throne are seven lamps, and in the center and around the throne are four living creatures (vv. 4-7). The living creatures cry out unceasingly, "Holy, holy, holy, is the Lord God, the Almighty, who was and who is and who is to come" (v. 8). That depicts the unending, angelic worship of God (v. 9).

b) The redeemed

We see the worship of the redeemed in verses 10-11, where the twenty-four elders (who represent redeemed men) fall down before God and worship Him, saying, "Worthy art Thou, our Lord and our God, to receive glory and honor and power; for Thou didst create all things, and because of Thy will they existed, and were created."

2. Those on earth

a) The obedient

"Those . . . on earth" (Phil. 2:10) refers to us. As believers we submit to Christ as Lord and Savior (by God's wonderful grace). We have followed the pattern of Romans 10:9: "If you confess with your mouth Jesus as Lord, and believe in your heart that God raised Him from the dead, you shall be saved." The lordship of Christ and His resurrection are connected because the resurrection was the first step in the exaltation of Christ as Lord.

b) The disobedient

The disobedient on earth will also bow before Jesus Christ—but by compulsion. Second Thessalonians 1:7-9 says, "When the Lord Jesus shall be revealed from heaven with His mighty angels in flaming fire, [He will deal out retribution] to those who do not know God and to those who do not obey the gospel of our Lord Jesus. And these will pay the penalty of eternal destruction, away from the presence of the Lord and from the glory of His power."

When Jesus returns to subdue the earth, He will remove the wicked from the earth, cast them into hell, and establish His kingdom. His kingdom will consist of His own people—the sheep of Matthew 25:31-40. The goats of Matthew 25:31-46 will also bow to His lordship but will then be destroyed in "the eternal fire which has been prepared for the devil and his angels" (Matt. 25:41).

3. Those under the earth

"Under the earth" refers to hell, the place of eternal punishment, which is occupied by damned demons and men. They also will acknowledge the lordship of Christ —not by enjoying His reign but by bearing the unending expression of His wrath. First Peter 3:18-22 indicates that while His dead body hung on the cross and then lay in His tomb, Christ's spirit descended into the prison (hell—cf. 2 Pet. 2:4) where certain demons are bound. There He proclaimed His triumph over them.

As affirmed in Psalm 2, all the earth will belong to Christ (v. 8). Some will acknowledge Him as Lord willingly. Others will need to be broken with a rod of iron (v. 9).

C. What Is to Be Acknowledged

Jesus Christ is Lord of the universe. Therefore "every tongue should confess that Jesus Christ is Lord" (Phil. 2:11). To confess (Gk., *exomologētai*) means "to acknowledge," "affirm," or "agree." Everyone—damned demons, damned men, holy angels, glorified saints—will acknowledge that He is Lord. By "every tongue" Paul did not mean every physical tongue in every mouth but every language (Gk., *glōssa*). Another way to express the idea is to say that all rational beings will acknowledge His lordship.

History is moving toward the day when Jesus will be acknowledged by all as the supreme ruler of the universe. He already sits in that seat of power but has not yet brought the universe fully under His authority. We live in days of grace, during which He brings men and women to acknowledge Him as Lord willingly rather than by force. That Jesus is Lord is the most important confession of Christianity.

IV. THE PURPOSE OF CHRIST'S EXALTATION

The purpose of Christ's exaltation is to glorify God. Philippians 2:11 says Jesus will be acknowledged as Lord, "to the glory of God the Father." In Isaiah 45:5 God says, "I am the Lord, and there is no other; besides Me there is no God." None can be compared to God. He does not ask anyone for advice. He knows all and does exactly what He wants to do. All His purposes come to pass.

In light of who God says He is, one might assume that for everyone to bow to Jesus Christ and confess Him as Lord might be blasphemous. To so honor Christ would seem to put Him in competition with the Father.

But the mystery of the Trinity is that when the Son is glorified, the Father is glorified. Perfect glory given to the Son is perfect glory given to the Father. John 5:23 says the Father has given all judgment to the Son "that all may honor the Son, even as they honor the Father. He who does not honor the Son does not honor the Father who sent Him." That's why the Father said of Jesus, "This is My beloved Son, with whom I am well pleased; listen to Him!" (Matt. 17:5). When you believe in Jesus Christ and confess Him as Lord, you not only exalt the Son but you also exalt the Father. We are not called to worship God through Jesus; we are called to worship Jesus as God. There is no competition within the Trinity. The Father is exalted by what He accomplishes in the Son. They are one.

A. Romans 9:5—"Christ . . . is over all, God blessed forever." When Christ was declared the sovereign of the universe, God blessed Him forever.

B. 1 Corinthians 15:28—Christ will subdue everything in the universe. "And when all things are subjected to Him, then the Son Himself also will be subjected to the One who has subjected all things to Him, that God may be all in all." God is glorified in anything that exalts the Son.

C. John 13:31-32—"Now is the Son of Man glorified, and God is glorified in Him; if God is glorified in Him, God will also glorify Him in Himself." The glory of the Father and of the Son are inextricably tied together.

Conclusion

The truths of Philippians 2:5-11, though a marvelous description of the saving work of Christ, primarily illustrate the need for humility in the Christian walk. A compelling reason for each believer to emulate the humility of Christ is the knowledge that it will bring about exaltation by God the Father. He who exalted His Son will exalt you. The humiliation and exaltation of Jesus Christ are not only the greatest truths in history but also a constant reminder of the fact that if we humble ourselves by seeking unity in the church, God will lift us up.

Focusing on the Facts

1. What is the only proper response to Christ's exaltation (see p. 57)?
2. The reason Christ was given His new name was to put Him in _____ (see p. 57).
3. Salvation is for those who confess Jesus as _____ (see p. 57).
4. What was God's expressed purpose in His exaltation of Christ (see p. 58)?
5. The phrases "every knee should bow" and "every tongue should confess" are taken from Isaiah 45:23. What does that text strongly emphasize (see p. 58)?
6. How does one receive the gift of salvation (see p. 59)?
7. According to Paul, who will bow the knee and confess that Jesus Christ is Lord (see p. 59)?
8. Who are "those . . . in heaven" referred to in Philippians 2:10 (see pp. 59-60)?
9. Why are the lordship of Christ and His resurrection connected (Rom. 10:9; see p. 60)?
10. Will those who are disobedient acknowledge that Jesus Christ is Lord? Why or why not (see pp. 60-61)?

11. To what does the phrase "under the earth" (Phil. 2:10) refer (1 Pet. 3:18-22; 2 Pet 2:4; see p. 61)?
12. When Paul said that every tongue would confess Christ, what did he mean (see pp. 61-62)?
13. It is a mystery of the Trinity that when the Son is glorified, what happens (see p. 62)?
14. What is a necessary part of the gospel invitation (see p. 62)?
15. What is one compelling reason for each believer to emulate the humility of Christ (see p. 63)?

Pondering the Principles

1. More than one hundred years ago in the book *Holiness: Its Nature, Hindrances, Difficulties, and Roots,* Anglican bishop J. C. Ryle wrote, "Doctrine is useless if it is not accompanied by a holy life. It is worse than useless: it does positive harm" ([Welwyn, Hertfordshire: Evangelical Press, 1979], p. xvii). Ryle was convinced that a prevalent problem in the church of his time was an unbiblical view of sin. His prescription: "We must sit down humbly in the presence of God, look the whole subject [of sin] in the face, examine clearly what the Lord Jesus calls sin, and what the Lord Jesus calls doing His will" (p. 13). Many in our day who profess to be Christians are unwilling to examine themselves for sin (2 Cor. 13:5) and to conform to the will of Jesus as Lord. Do you understand the hideous nature of sin in the sight of God and therefore the need to avoid it?

2. A major theological issue of our time concerns whether faith in Christ necessarily requires evident repentance from sin. Some have said that to require repentance of sin as a part of the gospel message—and as a ground of assurance of saving faith—is a form of legalism. Yet the first sermon of Christ was, "Repent, for the kingdom of heaven is at hand" (Matt. 4:17). Among His final words were, "Repentance for forgiveness of sins should be proclaimed in His name to all nations, beginning from Jerusalem" (Luke 24:47). The apostles also emphasized repentance: when Peter was asked what his hearers needed to do to be saved, he said, "Repent, and let each one of you be baptized in the name of Jesus Christ for the forgiveness of your sins" (Acts 2:38). Does repentance characterize your life? Do you realize its necessity for a daily walk with Christ?

Scripture Index

Topical Index

Moulton, James Hope, on
  morphē, 10

Repentance, importance of, 64
Resurrection, the. *See* Jesus
  Christ
Ryle, J. C., on examining one-
  self, 64

Service. *See* Meeting needs
Seven sayings on the cross. *See*
  Crucifixion
Sin, seriousness of, 24, 30, 64
Smith, Henry, on the honor of
  humility, 50

Spring, Gardiner, on the emblem of the cross, 21
Spurgeon, Charles Haddon
  on human glory, 35
  on the lordship of Christ, 50

Tozer, A. W, on the lordship of
  Christ, 46

Watson, Thomas, on the humility of love, 21
Worship, of Jesus Christ. *See* Jesus Christ